This Book Belongs To:

____

BY
Home Planners And
Journals
To help you organize your life